not one bit of this is your fault

Trent Busch

ISBN: 978-93-88125-84-0

Cover Artist: Faye Altman
Photograph: James Carper

First Edition: 2019
Rs. 200/-

Cyberwit.net
HIG 45 Kaushambi Kunj, Kalindipuram
Allahabad - 211011 (U.P.) India
http://www.cyberwit.net
Tel: +(91) 9415091004 +(91) (532) 2552257
E-mail: info@cyberwit.net

Printed at Repro India Limited.

To Carol who never, not one time, lost faith

Author's Note

not one bit of this is your fault is a book wherein each poem uses a woman as its subject. It is divided into four sections, each beginning with one poem based on a woman from mythology or the classics; the rest of the poems follow the theme of the first poem that begins each section. For example, the first section is called Aberration and the first poem's title is "Drusilla," (whose brother was Caligula), whereas the rest of the women in the section are more or less modern women. The next three sections follow this format.

The title comes from the 1996 novel *The Divine Secrets of the Ya-Ya Sisterhood* by Debra Wells when "Buggy" tells her granddaughter, Sidda, "not one bit of this is your fault".

At its heart, *not one bit of this is your fault* is a feminist book. Only in the last butterfly of time have most men attended women with dignity. I remember my grandfather dealt with my grandmother as one might deal with a troublesome pet that has become annoying. I never saw her sit down at the same table to eat with him.

The men in my family were not noble models at treating women fairly. Human tyranny cannot be conceived simply. Only recently have we become sensitive to our injustice and only recently have women's rights been taken seriously; we still have a long way to go.

Acknowledgments

Thanks to the editors of the following publications where poems, sometimes with different titles and in different form, first appeared:

Amoskeag: "Balanced at Forty."
Barkeater: The Adirondack Review: "Mrs. Hollister."
The Best American Poetry, 2001: "Heartland."
Blue Unicorn: "The Bun."
Carolina Quarterly: "Clorice Henry."
Chase Park: "Hilda."
The Chicago Review: "Reunion."
College English: "Elena," "St. Louis," and "Woman Asleep in a Chair."
Colorado State Review: "The Ducks."
Commonweal: "The Jilting of Mary Brown."
Confrontation: "Summer Day."
Cottonwood: "Clemson's Wife."
Cottonwood Retrospective: "Clemson's Wife."
Crazyhorse: "Drusilla."
Cumberland Poetry Review: "Girl in a Play."
The Evansville Review: "Drawing in Pencil."
Folio: "Girl Walking."
The Georgia Review: "My Old German Grandmother."
Great Midwestern Review: "Alcove."
Grasslimb: "Grandmother's Marriage."
Habersham Review: "Country House."
Hawai'i Review: "Portrait."
The Hudson Review: "Clytemnestra at the Palace Wall," "The Woman in the Window" and "Near Hickory."
Jabberwock: "Woman Away."

The Kenyon Review: "Newspaper Photograph" and "The Vase of Flowers."
Limestone: "Tia."
Manoa: "Dora Ann."
The Moth: "Pretty as it Is."
The Nation: "Heartland."
Natural Bridge: "Dawn Mountain Fog."
The Nebraska Review: "Romance."
New Orleans Review: "The Wake."
New York Quarterly: "For All the Miles."
North Dakota Review: "The Woman of Long Fingers."
Notre Dame Review: "Jilted Lady, Gold-Haired Lover" and "Stabbing."
Pleiades: "Cressida."
Poet and Critic: "The Clay."
Poetry, "Woman in a Swing" and "Aletha."
Red Rock Review: "The Undeserving."
River Styx: "The Singer."
Rockhurst Review: "Going West."
So It Goes, The Literary Journal of the Kurt Vonnegut Museum and Library, "Viagra."
Spillway: "Peaches."
Spire Magazine: "Woman at Blackwater Falls."
Steam Ticket: "Funeral."
Sundog: The Southeast Review: "The Hunter's Wife."
Tar River Poetry: "A Show about Nothing."
Third Coast: "The Scythe."
Threepenny Review: "Lost, Perhaps in London."
Zone 3: "Copperhead."

Contents

III. REBELLION

IV. ADORATION

I. Aberration

DRUSILLA

We walked the tangled hill
and crossed the deep gorge
on the invisible bridge
and spent our day
above the blue valley.

If he was my lover,
he was my brother too,
my father, the other half
of self that made me
that egg impervious
to any serpent's tooth.

Could I say, I would name
the origin of needs
that brought fear and horror
in those others' eyes
who would have died
before they would have borne
what I loved.

Only he could break me,
shackled, willing, tame,
or know there was
no Roman way,
though Rome came closest,
to measure passion,

and only he knew
what I had become,
what together we had made
that was more than he,
Rome, or any god could be,

that the screams
were not our screams
but of a voice beyond Olympus
that, dying, would neither
spill nor bleed, nor leave
a trace of ashes
upon the desperate floor.

FOR ALL THE MILES

How can we guess, knowing
little of their history,
what women of genius
felt in those days

when they looked out
at nightfall over their
husbands' fields, feeling
their bodies heavy with

another child, knowing
the absence of softness,
of tenderness the stern land
could not seed or allow?

how their youthful tears in
middle afternoons were
their only repose in
days filled with duty when

for all the miles theirs was
the single woman's voice
to soothe the outlaw wind?
until hearts took on what

cannot be written, strength
men dismiss as madness,
mouths lined with nothing
more to fear but the last

gift in a person's life,
like the she-wolf exiled
from the pack, voice high,
eyes closed against the moon.

NEWSPAPER PHOTOGRAPH

She watches the sky, holding
her hat against a forties
wind, her heavy coat pressed
against a rope-lined street,

her other hand shading
her eyes from the winter
sun, saying goodbye to some
diminishing hope:

caught there the tear in heart
the bird knows held in the soft
mouth of the cat, the ear
knows when the sound bone breaks.

In dots and space, it is
too what we do not see,
crowd dispersed, the wound up
rope, her same bound figure

seeking comfort along
a wind-swept street, that makes
us want to alter what
the picture has left out,

expose and substitute,
meddle in endings, to

take her hand and see her
safely home, to banish

cession in the captured
bird and the fractured bone.

DORA ANN

A wild ringing in the summer
air, the road turns and turns; Uncle
Jim is dead, Madge Burch grows larger
and larger. The fit is on Jean.

False steps as the child holds the doll
closer; no one can say the word
to stop her rocking and staring
as the walls fly past the window.

Take her limp hand, it does no good;
touch her forehead, it is normal.
Send her brother to the store for
potatoes. Will she go with him?

"I want to go home." "But you are
home, dear." "I want to go home."
"Keep her from the news," Aunt Irma
says. "Events are stuffing her head."

At last something sane. "Where then is
home, my darling?" A butterfly
on the wild iris. Rocked in the lap
of the rabbit's apron, without dream.

She does not stop, she will never
stop. She feels no hunger, threat of
danger, no desire or anger,
no prompting at her mother's grief.

THE SINGER

They clap for her as if
she is what they came
to see, not the smoke
that rises like blue fog

on a morning river or
pain that makes her throat
tremble or sounds that
sting or drunken air.

The singer does not hear
or see the faces or hear
her own voice, only pain
or joy or mixing of joy

and pain together as she
remembers once when she
sat watching in a motel
mirror her lover leaving.

It is not the song they
love, but the singer,
not the lights that change
from city to city;

it is she they love as
her words become theirs, who
weave a circle round her,
singing to themselves.

STABBING

Three or four cows and a house
make a farm when you walk
in Brohard, painter-wise.

Never mind limestone rocks
covered with loose dirt for
stalls in barns—or the flies.

Three or four purple flowered
weeds and a butterfly
make a field, never mind

the basket on a mussy
quilt thrown beneath a tree
on poor grass—or the fence.

The woman who stabbed her
lover and his wife must have
said, Never mind the blood;

three or four moments of
silence and a sigh make
the mind paint, killer-wise.

ELENA

Wind has wrenched a limb from
the old oak and thrust
it like an arm across
the row of boxwoods. Rain

is lashing north in an
uncustomary way
as the hurricane, mad
Elena, routs the gulf.

How you differed from this
storm that is your name,
tearless the whole week when
your mother died, buying

groceries, back and forth
to the station, walking
quietly beneath the giant
trees without a coat.

"She will weep later," your
brother said, gaunt
and nodding, but no one
ever saw you prove him right.

Few of us know how others
turn out, whom we see maybe
twice a lifetime after,
but here today your namesake

brings you through the years
into this weather that now
whispers and ceases, then like
an outraged lover pounds

the windows and screams like
a child across the night.

THE CLAY

At first the clay was square;
she shaped it, then kneaded
it as if it were dough
and dressed it as a pastry.

She wrapped it, then hid it
behind a box of salt
and took it out only
when she was lonely.

One day she dressed it in
a tie and showed it off
behind big windows, she
took it home to mother.

This is the clay you have
heard me speak of, she said.
She teased it to be sure
that it was not happy.

When it came home drunk, she
taught it the lesson of
the knocked off hat, of the
dog in the flower bed.

She told the clay it could
be a cigarette if
it wished, but it could be
a coffin somewhere else.

After it was soiled, she
grew weary, though some days
she pretended the dream
of the rough package; she

rolled it to the fragrance
of ginger and visited
her mother, seasoning
that she would not unlearn.

GIRL IN A PLAY

Dressed in the old ones' clothes,
she crosses the stage, bent
in a stubborn walk, playing
make-believe with anger;

for an hour the body
believing in itself,
tuck of hips lost, heavy
waist, the sweet breast fallen.

Then in the city park
the morning after, spring
in the green leaves, studying
again the old ones coming

to their benches, the fire
lost and regained and lost
once more in their final
conversations, learning

their speech and movement as
the wind whispers and lake
water rocks the returning
ducks, yet guards its secret.

Youth knows what the young know
the old have forgotten;
if old age howls, it comes
with that keen punishment.

MRS. HOLLISTER

Whether she has lost
her mister
or the opal ring
her mother gave her
or her cat,

Mrs. Hollister
will tear the tile
from the solid floor
or sling the hinges
from the gate,

then roll a birdbath
down the yard
or flush
a careless duck
into the lake.

Comfort!
What is that but some
wagging mouths trying
to get themselves,
not her, peace?

None of it.
Passion must be spent:
"Injustice or bad luck,
call it the stepping down
or up of events,

"inevitable
and to be met with
the proper outfling
into the idea of
whatever blackguard face."

Later, on another
floor and still unspent
she sobs
and pounds the carpet
with one fist.

Watching is past,
behind her the darkening
squares of glass
and sparked above her life
a burning sourceless blaze.

THE VASE OF FLOWERS

Arrangement is an accident,
she said, turning from the vase of
flowers, relying on roadside reds
or blues or hillside yellows then
in season,
just as the town ripped
in two by the tornado might
have been a Virginia showcase
for nineteenth century architecture.

He said, Well they are beautiful,
though she did not need to destroy
a town for their sake, perhaps more
lovely without topography.

As mood too has direct effect,
she said, the way the hand and eye
control tone or the way we sit
together alone at coffee.

So there is more than nature or
desire, she said, as if country
girls could on looks alone arrive
bare-armed in bright regalia
at the ball,
or gentlemen with fine
words rise to power were they not
by melancholy smile or glance
of flashy dress too much distracted.

He said, I can see what you are
getting at, though she need not bring
in the male's penchant for sex when
flowers were equally stunning.

An accident, as simple as
that, she said. We trust too much to
genius, expecting to flourish for
years what may bloom its one first time.

A VISIT FROM THE MUSE

We both know you need no door to
enter, so sit down, over there
if you wish, let me have a look
at you. Yes, yes, that's much better.

Now, let's see. Perhaps we can go
ahead and start; I know how you
like ready visits. No, no notes;
yes, you're far too edgy for that.

Well, if it's only about your
sisters. I'm going to need more
than this. We've worn that tale to
near perfection. The role's full up.

I sense we're getting something here:
you've had remorse? not being used
but using? Well, if not breakthrough,
something. What, already you're going?

Yes, I know that. Oh, I'm not worried
about the money. Sure, I'll be
careful and observe your warning:
can never tell when we might be had.

SISTERS

No one seemed to notice, or mind,
that she stayed on the fringe of things,
dangling her feet from a rock by
the river where we others swam,

only her sister understanding
her words, leading her up the slick
bank, helping with her shoes, brushing
leaves and mud from her legs and skirt.

School the same, standing far enough
from danger to avoid the bounding
ball, the uncontrollable, wild
bodies trampling the school yard.

Or question or imagine her thoughts
as she gazed at the honking geese,
then, after rain, stooped to return
earthworms from the sidewalk to the grass.

As if we knew we could not trip
the bolt if we dared, to lead her
across twilight to, for what was
us, the bright star of adulthood,

leaving it to her sister to
help her cross into her body's
center, teaching and learning herself
from the passage how not to fail.

THE BUN

There is no having fun
in this life,
tight spooled, pinned,
barretted,
moving with the strict nose
of the library countenanced.

If I work loose enough
at mid-morning
to summon the glance
of a stranger
I am tucked and powdered
as if I were a child.

And by afternoon, many times
poked with pencils,
harassed by glasses,
I am stayed tighter
than a girdle on someone's
great-aunt Grundella.

Evenings out, it is
uptight all over again,
even if
the long-stemmed drinking
elicits only a shrug
for straying.

What joy is there spilled
alone on a chair?
I would talk to Cleopatra,
the blond on the corner.
Effete? No, a curl
in a world with no horrid.

OF HEIGHT AND DEPTH

The moment came and was gone.
It would not come again.
Not that moment. It was gone.

So she took from some old drawer
something. Something. It was
nothing to do physical harm.

Had it been, the moment
might still have been alive.
It was nothing to care about.

There was no garden outside
and no warm sun to shine
on a path through cedars.

Without limousine or gown
she did not stop to think
what it takes for tragedy,

nor, though she might shape
the word, sensibility,
nor dignity in mourning.

How far then was this room,
this nothing in this wooden
drawer, from one nobly born,

who through brush or poem, in
spite of moment come and gone,
might have become through

a labyrinth of chances, even
with branded neck or hand,
a fabled dryad cast in bronze.

II. Irresolution

PENELOPE

What woman could guess, secure in
father's arms, the distant glance,
sullenness of face time drapes
over men's eager eyes?

And what woman not fooled?
living on memory: that first year
when lust, time's only enemy,
kept his heart strong for only me.

Only with Antinous, my body
young and introduced to love,
could I guess the mortal
blood of Odysseus, the want

in the suitor's eyes reminding his,
the understanding, the patience,
all the while making his own
journeys in my handmaidens' beds.

Oh, I know in my husband's mind,
minds of all green men, he was
faithful, loyal to a breathless
shape that did not wake or eat,

and even with Circe, Calypso,
all those changeless sirens, he,
like all green men, did nothing
to warrant shame in Ithaca.

At first I thought so too:
the night we had that night;
throat-frozen cries, finished
at last the shroud of Laertes.

But then nights when he called out
names I thought forgotten, dawn
still dreaming, the long walks,
the day he was utterly alone.

The awful way he looks out at
the sea. Was there this for me
to know: figures at the loom learn
equally the designs of gods?

And must I wait again, to die
that secret I came to be, steadfast
stance, immovable bed built
into the trunk of living tree?

HEARTLAND

And she saying, I cannot quite
hear what she says, but he, standing
in clothes washed too often still
to be warm, looks out at the land.

And she saying, I cannot hear
what follows his name, and he, "What's
it all meant, Lizzie? We've made
a living and no one doubts our name."

And he remembering the years
before the green combines and long,
open barns for machinery
and their hands on each other young.

And she saying, I cannot tell
whether or not it's comforting,
until he turns to a door that
is not a new house and goes in.

And she saying, I can hear now,
"If the words are old, let them be.
It's hard enough with a dream;
here, what can you see of a plan?"

And he nodding, I can no longer
hear what she says, the house shadowed
by combines and long open barns,
the fields planted and bare for rain.

CLORICE HENRY

Well, I'm proud to be
a coal miner's daughter,

—Loretta Lynn

Doing the work of a
man. Handling the reins,
building the load,
stacking the hay as well
as ever Zebe could.

Replacing window panes,
hanging a screen door,
putting new boards on
the porch, I haven't
worn a dress in months,
only own one decent one.

We do as we can, him
gone mostly, working in
the mine, black as a
burned stump. Can never
get the sheets clean.

I have heard the song
by Loretta Lynn. I
would like a chance
to sing about a woman

in this hollow. About
hardships and pleasures.

A song about a dress.
A brooch. A small church,
a burial. Pride is
sweat. About a woman
who could taste the mouth
of God easier than
imagine a million dollars.

THE DUCKS

Light pales. I wade
with the ducks
evening after evening
at the creek,
waiting for him
to pass, to light
a wish my way.

Often on the bus
when I was ten and
he was high school's
tight-hipped hero
I bared my eyes
to his sure face.

Now I am shier,
gathering my dress
below my knees,
casting bread crumbs
on the water.

Oh, there's a husband
on this place,
a belt-bellied man
with easy hands who
makes the farm work.

Not the ducks.
Belonging to no one,

even the farm. Head
first in the water.

Red. His truck and
my face turning away.
Again, not one glance,
as if he sees all
the work he's left
behind ahead to do.

These ducks. Could he
know how I envy them.
Diving into a darkness
they are sure of.

THE WOMAN IN THE WINDOW

Just once I wish he'd walked
through the house at noon
in nothing but his shorts
and made me put my book down.

When he did come home for lunch,
all he'd do is enter
through the back door and eat
what I'd fixed without a word.

I was never modern; a career
was something I didn't have,
not something taken from me;
he made money, so I didn't.

I don't miss him really,
not a man at table, not
his fume of smoke vanishing
and being there again.

What I miss is times prettier
than they were, like the times
that hadn't happened yet when
I was a girl, looking out

the window of my room
on a summer night imagining
how I'd feel if I was
married and my husband died.

PEACHES

Make the words hard, Elizabeth,
hard as nails that hold together doors
exposed to weather fifty years.

Him. Such demands are the ice
that bends the limbs and makes them beg
to break like shards upon the ground.

Once, in spring, when youth was firm
against my blouse, I took him
places he could not live without;

now, the road bends back upon
itself and everything I say
is nonsense against argument.

Whatever time it is, it is
the wrong time; I can't bear to
look at any clock, trying hard

to stay away from anything
that might contain myself, lest it
be true that he is normal and I

am normal, and these trees, empty
now, normal, that have it in
themselves to bloom and end and bloom.

HILDA

He came round the corner
of my daddy's house with
blue-jeaned leg and tractored
skin, asking for my hand

like someone he had read
about, as if an okay
to that made my head nod
too, amazed that, though we

(true) had done more than smell
the honeysuckle, I
might dare to be a fool
outside that pastoral.

Like the blackbird I am
of three minds, feeling
the flutter of genes to
dally in the green wind,

adopt a plot of ground,
feed mouths that while I grow
thin, on feathered legs
they can test their wings,

or preen night's plumage
and by day catch the draft
of blue air, soar above
fence lines, old songs with old

design, and at summer's
end glide across burning
fields to be the single
bright eye in winter's wind.

NEAR HICKORY

For a week now he has
not started his truck, back
and forth in a cold month
from barn to house, causing
her to say he might at
least go to the store and loaf.

There is no word again
today and as they sit
they wonder if what
the correspondent on
TV said was true: some
do not want to come back.

Her cousin's boy had been
killed outright and when they
brought the flagged box
into the church she got no
farther in her thoughts than
the shine on the soldier's boots.

She thought now about her
own boy's shoes and how each
morning after breakfast
and before the bus, he
shined them between his knees
and held them to the light.

She cannot remember
what she wanted for him then
or if she can she has
put it with old pieces
she used to save for quilts
on some forgotten shelf.

And what Webb thought, well
what man wasn't he like,
switching stations on and off
and talking gruff, wondering
if what the missing wished
is what those wishing do.

DRAWING IN PENCIL

It was not smoke, she said, not the smoke
of cigarettes that hung in the room,
the room of a restaurant, perhaps,
with rich tile floor and orchestra.

It was not cigarette smoke, the way
that she could tell it, not the smoke
from fires, not wood smoke, not smoke
from chimneys as it hung there in curls,

as it hung there a few feet above
the diners' heads, the women in
long-armed dresses, sequined, with
an orchestra on a dais behind.

More a mist, she said, rising at dawn
over water, but not mist exactly,
more structured than mist, hanging in
a layer of not exactly curls

over the diners' heads, as if
there were no men at all, though there
were, of course, there were most certainly
men, just as now he was a man

listening and she trying to
describe the wisps that hung in the room
a few feet above their heads or
if they stood, their heads and mist one,

how the mist did not matter, whether
from floor angle or orchestra dais,
how it could not be told the way
she saw it, to him or from herself.

SUMMER DAY

I wipe the crumbs
from the oil cloth
into my hand.
I put the blue bowl
into the cupboard.
Summer blows past
the sunlit windowsill.

He has been watching
in my thoughts
for weeks. Trying to
coax me to meet him
at the beech tree
by the creek. Seeing
beneath my dress
and beckoning.

I will not come,
I say, keeping my
steps busy, turning
from his voice
and again and again
from his face.

Sometimes the walls
break, sometimes,
heartbeat, I pull
his mouth to mine,

then drop a dish the
rattle of a snake.

If thoughts were scenes,
get out, get out,
the fever of my breath,
don't speak, my life
an easy-needing man.

There. Myself again.
Cold sweat in these
summer days for weeks.
How long until and can
it be this season breaks
or I stray into his
thoughts watching him?

WOMAN ASLEEP IN A CHAIR

Variation on Renoir's *Sleeping Girl*

One hand limp in the lap
of her blue skirt, head tilting,
the other resting wrist
down past the wine cushion.

Legs slanting, one foot drawn
under as if on command
she might rise and take
saucers from the cupboard.

Breasts green pears, the strap
on her white blouse, fallen
on her shoulder, has rolled
into a lace garter.

No one can stop the passion
on her mouth, or innocence,
upper lip pouting,
bottom straight with shyness.

Final glance at the hands
surrenders her difference,
not of a lady, though
maybe a lady's hands,

that might yet know wealth
and a gentleman's kindness,
but keep her in blouses
and betray her in sleeping.

CLEMSON'S WIFE

Another move, another borrowed
truck, boxing rags that were already
rags when we blew another breath
into another broken house.
Sweeping glass, cardboard tacked on missing
windowpanes, pretending the first
week that hammering can lean it straight.

Why do I stay with a man always
out of work, or when he finds a job,
sleeping in the first dark day of rain,
coming home the following noon
saying, "I can't work for that man."

I ask myself that question every
day. Always the fight, the make up.
Another job, then the wailing
walls and a ghost child on my hip.

I know what people say, what I
would say and probably did as
a small child growing up, about
the trash that loads their trash into
a borrowed pickup truck and moves
to a place already left as lost.

But now I stop and take one
final look, the kids hollering
and Clemson yelling, "Hurry up."

Here and foolish, am I not allowed
to know what others know: that part
of me is taken there, that all
the world is older, that I stay
because of some place else to go.

WOMAN AT BLACKWATER FALLS

A mile from the highway
now, climbing with the road
to the top of mountain
where oaks signal their arms
like an old man waving.

Over the edge the slope
falls to a dry gully,
but I hear, hidden by
laurel, the white rush of
water deep in the gorge.

Not that I do not want
him, not that my heart
does not push blood like a
falling stream, crashing deep,
swollen and deafening.

But I have stopped on
this mountain where oaks are
waving and the yellow
road is curving behind me.
And will go no further.

For then I am lost, the
I like a butterfly
flown from my mouth, the
me of myself aloft
in claws to be swallowed.

What I wanted was words
to breathe; with him there was
no breathing. I don't know
if there is with any
man. What I wanted was

submerging, then lying
cleansed, the way that shadows
close the evening of a
farm. What I wanted was
a man that left me whole.

A COUNTRY HOUSE

Waking, she felt the wind
from late summer blowing
through the open window.

A lone dog barked somewhere,
and she remembered how
on such a day when she

was a child her mother
had awakened her to tell
her that her aunt was dead.

Rising, a flannelled shirt
about her shoulders, she
picked up her brush from the

mirrored table, took it
with her to the open
window and looked out at

the browning green of the low
hills and thought of how
her aunt had loved ballet.

Staring, she could see her
still, dancing the low hills
and promising a trip

to the great city where
they would sit in white gloves
and tight-sleeved dresses to

watch how by a ruse an
English fortune hunter
ruined a Russian princess.

Brushing, she knew now no
such ballet had ever
existed, yet how her

wariness of men still
persisted because of that
rich mind that fed upon

a wind from some late
summer with every good
intent to please a child.

ST. LOUIS

Meet me in St. Louis, Louie,
Meet me at the fair.

She awakes and walks to
the hotel window and looks
down upon the vacant
tables, the still pool,
and thinks of his words, the way
that he said she would do.

From a drawer she takes
a postcard with a picture
of her room and writes,

"Today here in St. Louis,
in St. Louis here today,
today I thought of you."

How the mornings change,
the lines around the mouth
grow deeper, words with wine,
drunk with laughter, a vase
of flowers, how suddenly
one day the lies are true.

It is noon. He brought her
nothing but happiness
and danger; she tears the card
in two. In the lobby

she meets no strangers, no
intrigue in the business room.

Outside, it is autumn
and shadows cool the streets
along the river. Then
darkness as lights begin
to shine on St. Louis
and night waits for the fair.

WOMAN IN A SWING

She dabs at her eyes,
sitting the porch swing,
and stares at the ridge
green-backed against
the sky.
                    She does not
know I watch, by chance
on a rise near the
garden, but I know
what has happened:

and who will fix the
faucet now when it
drips, drips long into
the night and replace
the burned-out light on

the cellar stairs? Who
will tramp with wet and
muddy feet and throw
carrots on the table?
Who will fix the lock?

Taken care of all her
life as if she were
a summer queen, her
audience is gone, the
forsaken garden dumb.

For this she weeps in
silence there and stares
at hills as young as
days when she still was
young, when
                    she loved a
man, when she would have
broken the rocky
field and slept on straw
had he but let her.

III. Rebellion

CLYTEMNESTRA AT THE PALACE WALL

Tell me what sins he did
not commit. Let's start with
one pretty one nudged a
windless dawn to shiny death
to please an impish goddess.

For what? Did I not know
better than anyone
the tramp the dullard his
aging brother could not
in peacetime keep at home?

Listen to pleas? He heard
no one, licensed to sail
and kill and carouse with
anyone his new-gained
generalship could win.

With trinkets and baubles,
with beard soft and black and
assuring, he seduced
all of my own toward
a hatred deeper than blood.

And that other one, her
sluttish face brown, hair bleached
lying the afternoon
deck the months coming home,
her nightly comforting.

See the whore! down the foolish
streets of Argos, arguing,
bracelets torn from her arms
as she is cast into
the crowd, the smile on his wide

face as he climbs the marble
steps, hands raised and turning,
his dark head streaked with gray,
that has grown no wiser,
that will grow no older.

THE JILTING OF MARY BROWN

Telling the woman easily
and politely she could not sleep
in the barn, the last man nearly
burning it down, flipping
a cigarette into the straw.

Could tell she smoked, yellow
stains on her hands and in spite
of her shape would have to be firm.

As easily and politely she
shot the short-barreled gun,
twice in the chest and the soft
pool of blood under the
porch light outside his door.

Prison then, child grown to
become prince of forlorn, her
not knowing why he would give

her no room, and the tall
father gone who would bring her
rich presents should she remain
true and raise her a kingdom
and scent it with myrrh.

THE WAKE

I lived 900 years
with the old bastard
and now he's dead,
leaving me here
with gray pubic hair
and a fallen vagina.

I forgave him everything:
that hussy heifer
who pissed away
his whole month's check
at Bill's Beer Joint,

the hunting trip
where he didn't just
not kill a deer
but shot off half his hand
in the bargain,

the evening he handed
me his work pants
and told me to grow
a set of balls
when I told Jake and Sam

he wasn't playing poker
until he planted
at least one field
of corn for the stock—

but those things
weren't a blighted tomato
compared to this:
died with me asleep
in the same bed.

He never had consideration.
If I had him back
I'd croak him myself,
going off to hell
like that and leaving me
here with no one
to cry at my funeral.

BALANCED AT FORTY

Children now and the dream
gone of whatever career:
acting, perhaps, or golden
playgirl with long legs on

beaches to stop men's hands
at castles and make them
rise from their white deserts
and drink at her oasis.

Beds to make now, toilets,
if still the modern woman,
managing the savings
and loan, showing houses,

or teaching one-minded
Juliets and Romeos
too mean to understand
youth in their nurse's tone.

With one doing his best
to be the modern man,
fumbling his breakfast, her
red, Saturday night plans,

but still with old demands,
shirts and hurts and lost keys
and love, needs to him as
natural as daffodils.

Balanced at forty, looking
back at days that stream
away like landscape from
a flying window, she

sees before her all their
wishes, the flood of rain
against her forward glass,
dusk, the wipers slashing.

THE SCYTHE

The scythe is still.
Its point is upward,
sharpened, its snath
balanced against a tree.

The day is noon.
It cannot take
its face from its hands,
shadowed in the sun.

The scythe has no
remorse. The grass lies
curing on the ground.

The heel it rests
on is cast iron;
the point is upward,
the hay is curing.

The day is a woman
with her face between
her hands. The night
might be a man.

The scythe leans against
a tree. The grass
is down. There is
no rumor of wind
and no bird song.

THE HUNTER'S WIFE

"You want excitement.
I'll give you blood."
Screen door slam.
The trees
dripping in autumn.

I never said excitement,
not that word,
change either, though
that is as close
as any word I meant—

dragging in stories
of patience,
"not an eye blink
if the rifle will
find the buck's heart."

Everything rote, ritual.
The second I would
prefer had it running
blood in it. Maybe
the word was mine.

I do not miss mornings
he spends in the sights
of his gun—God knows
the peace his rounds
bring this house.

It's off the track
I mean, not
bagged like an animal.
What I want to say
is not love:

he is full of that.
What I want to say
is to be shot free,
winged somewhere,
not the certain kill.

GIRL WALKING

The girl in blue smock walks
at daybreak below stout
trees on the asphalt road.

She does not whistle, nor
talk to herself, eyes straight,
arms swinging fluidly.

She has awakened dogs
and startled the roosting
birds in the thick branches.

She knows but would not say
what else she will startle;
today she goes to the store.

Her grandmother walked this
road before her mother.
She will meet no strangers.

No one walks with her on
the asphalt road, her list
tucked into her blue smock.

She walks straight and her brown
shoes are comfortable;
she does not fear the dogs.

She understands the quietness
of the road, the long shadows
below the thick branches.

She knows and walks directly:
the sun is not yet hot
and she is in no hurry.

MY OLD GERMAN GRANDMOTHER

My old German grandmother
bombed out of Hamburg, asked,
"Are you religious?" answers,
stern across the cheek bones,
"My lineage, my name, my house
it is boomed, poof! The father
of my six children is five
years in Siberia—comes home
broken to die in my arms.
My children they starve. And should
I go to my knees for food?
No Jesus bread man gives outside
my door. What good miracles?
With these two hands I feed.
I raise them right. They make
me no trouble. I teach them good
from bad. No stealing. No cursing
in my house. They have the respect,
the pride. No, I do not believe."

REUNION

They are having a reunion
in the big house in the bottom.
No kin of mine, though old Johnson,
up the hollow yesterday checking
cattle, invited me to come.

I'll think about it, I said. What
family of mine would spit twice
to see my suitcase thrown before
me at their door. What family
either would I spit twice to see.

Five years I have slept this trailer,
living off the money of a war
I always hated, paid to the wife
of a missing soldier whom I
never loved. I did not ask for

justice, though I take it, the check
coming every month. If only
they could know the civilians that
I wasted in my night battles
soliciting impossible divorce.

That is done. Old Johnson asking
no questions, always proper, as
if it is my fidelity
that reunions are built on. This
morning I thought I might go down:

long tables built among the oaks
along the drive, heavy baskets
and checkered tablecloths, life or
death tag between the dusty cars,
men's cries and the ring of horseshoes.

Ten years since I got the letter.
What could I give there, what would they
give me? Woman in a trailer,
unrelated, alone, unwilling
to repent her ungratefulness.

ALCOVE

The simple way she looked
away from him and rose
and put the saucer in
the sink as if she had
found a bird's egg in the grass
and moved a branch and placed
it safely with the others.

Never to see again,
not studying the outcome—
the neighbor's cat, the young
boy's pellet, the still-born
embryo—things unimportant
to the act that came to
her naturally as loving.

As finished as that, she
scraped the dishes, he said
his word, left, and outside
on the patio the tail
of the neighbor's cat twitched
once before he looked up
and meowed at the window.

Dishes started, she looked
out on the garden. Between
the cedar and hedge
a bird had fallen. Glass
reflected what she knew
had started. Nor heard when
the cat meowed again.

VIAGRA

You'd think God would let a man
rest and give a woman peace
after fifty years. Yet He's come
along (you feminists tell me now
He could be a woman) and dropped
a formula in some young (of course)
scientist's ear on how to raise
Mt. Richard from its limpid deep.

As if breakfast and underwear
and the weekly sweep were not enough,
now he's come squeezing and poking
his attention into every nook
a kitchen holds private, making
weekdays and chores already bad
worse with innuendoes about
weekend time trials and pole position.

I don't know what's to be done now
except to wish (you see the embarrassment
of prayer) that Nature, a woman herself,
somehow corrects the enormous
mistake by restoring to all of us
some intellect: why, from patriarch's
days it's been nothing but good sense
to leave the genitals blacked out.

JILTED LADY, GOLD-HAIRED LOVER

I felt the usual things when
he left—of course at the time I
didn't think they were usual—

then rounded out the baby part
of a year that ended with a short
man sweating and a wife in braces,

the woman across explaining
a desk full of papers that
precluded first words and visits,

normal stuff that takes most
of us down to empty beaches
and a sky full of screaming gulls.

You might say, though, if you've an ounce
of spite about you, things for me
turned out opposite and gladly.

Naturally, I am older, but I
have a late breakfasts, the ocean,
a slew of dresses in my closet.

Maybe the wife was only civic
minded, her short man become
a giant in a land of aisles,

maybe one stood from her basket
and nakedly and naturally
entered the world of apes and wolves.

PRETTY AS IT IS

Sometimes, instead of making
a jewelry box wouldn't it be
better just to have a good cry?

I mean, look at this; you've been
working on it for a month and it
still not finished, pieces all over

the table, your heart no better
than it ever was, and when
finished another one's to build.

What I'm saying is, crying has
closure: you bawl your eyes out for
an hour, then end with a hard sniffle.

Pretty as it is, what will you
have when it's done? Who'll buy it?
You said yourself it's for no one.

I swear whoever said women
are romantic ought to see you,
standing there looking like the last

thing you could ever do is hurt.
For god's sake, flinch. Let your hair
be all over your face one time.

GOING WEST

She unlocks the car door with no key,
the new-fashioned way, throws her coat
in back, puts her purse on the floor
of the front seat, and drives away.

No one's with her now, as surely
someone would have been a generation
earlier, as she set forth to cross
a country of what would then have

been mostly ordinary people
shocked at her bare leg on the top
step of a station where she'd pause for
rest and gas and Coca Cola.

Now she wears jeans on highways much
more hostile, the one behind her
not the first she's had to drive away
from to get over, nor the worst.

Before she's gone there will be many
fields of grain to wave, many signs
that will color the drab outskirts of
towns she'll both ignore and sleep in.

For just beyond the hood are lines
drawn that she guns over, erasing
doubt, guilt, taboos, and baggage, in
the old tradition, going west.

IV. Adoration

CRESSIDA

If I love him more than
I should, set it down
to overbearance, he
who threatens my balance

with his whole gesture,
eyes that smile through water,
set it down to assurance
that perseverance will

undo neither him nor me,
that he, fallen, and me
on my knees above him,
who has taken my sweetness,

silences me with silence,
dresses me brazenly
for rivals, fox across
a clearing in broad day.

If I love him more than
I should, set it down
to impatience, they
with their noisy chances,

more afraid to triumph
than to fail, set it down
to risk of breath, he who
breathes into my mouth

the mouth of rivers,
lost channels that when
he turns his watch away
I navigate alone.

But on this shore I stand:
vulnerable, dependent
as I am, stronger
without than within his arms.

COPPERHEAD

Down the path from the road
I come walking. Past the
barn toward the back door
of the house.
It is daylight,
and I have bunched my dress
for an hour now, my legs
wet from the night grass.

I have been bitten by
a snake, thick, copper-headed,
the wound swelling and my
flesh a dizzy pink.

Who cares what kind, the snake,
who cares who, the coil more
frightening than the strike,
a sip of venom

from a tall glass, a thrown
away doll I wanted
only yesterday. Just
these last steps,
the stairs to
reach, then past the burning
lamp in my mama's face
and I will not die.

TIA

Tia could never get the feel
for the country: bales of hay didn't
hook for her and anybody dumb
enough to ride a horse instead
of a Harley or Mercedes
deserved a thistle in the ass.

She rode down Fifth Avenue as if
Fifth Avenue existed only
to be ridden down, and how could
nights for locals compare to the stars
that danced behind glass windows?

Tia was her own world, everyone
knew that, and could make it big
even in a car wreck or on
a tabloid cover as the woman
behind some billion dollar heist.

How she looks old and what she thinks,
those with distance might say,
not we who were seconds to her
act, faint strokes in the background
of a picture's boldness, content
to be rehearsers of her song.

A SHOW ABOUT NOTHING

She takes something from her pocket
(we guess it to be a key),
gives whatever it is to him,
and we have a scene in the making.

Though too far away to tell exactly,
we think she has on a denim
jacket; what we enjoy most is not
knowing what's started or ending.

Those eager to know what happens,
in fact most of the audience,
will stop now, leave in a huff from
the theater, or else turn the pages,

though we think the weather is cold
from what we think is a jacket
and surely they must be young from
what we don't know of their motives.

Do we make it up and watch or
watch and make it up: three elements:
a girl, what we think is a key
from her jacket, his moment hers.

GRANDMOTHER'S MARRIAGE

It took him three hours to say here
they were again, night so black they
couldn't see the maps before their eyes.

The wind was blowing the harness reins
through the cracks in the barn and snow
was chamfering the calf pen fence.

It was a story they would tell,
mostly she and then she alone
after he died, to anyone

with a troubled marriage: how first
knots would tighten the rope on any
kind of second life, hard weather

but a winter mumbling, having
forgotten spring water and summer's
eyes with their paper lashes.

Get up any night with your flashlight
or your lantern, go to the kitchen
window and tell her what face you

could see looking in, your tears
drying, the hope that was still there
and the fear that would outlive you.

ROMANCE

Eager to know what it meant,
she read the letter over
and over, sitting in
a window seat in a blue
dress, watching the river.

Did it say come or stay?
and if it said come, would
she go and would she say
outright she was going
or take the cover of night?

In France once a woman
met a lover she did not
know and was soon destroyed,
her hat with green feathers
dropped and ruined in the rain.

But there was still the letter
and what did it mean with
its curving figures, its bold
assertions and withdrawing
warnings trailing the margin?

One day would rise with others,
and should she risk the weeks
and years that other women
took waiting for loves who
turned out to be husbands?

She was procrastinating
now and knew it and made
the decision she would not
make at thirty if only
she were seventeen again.

She chose the night of course,
slipping her flowered suitcase
into the trunk, her own driver,
speeding down the empty street,
wishing she had horses.

THE WOMAN OF LONG FINGERS

We of the long fingers,
hands that busy the cloth
awaiting the return
of the hero know small else,

but know the shadows of
the neglected room, stains
on the bare floor, darkened
by light from the lone window.

We know the cats that are
used to drowse all day soon
gone from boredom, their necks
lavished with amethysts,

and know the men with dark
hearts who would keep us here
and who try to deceive
us with seals and parchment.

We of the long fingers
live in high houses, chairs
niggard, lean dreams that wind
down to the rocky shore,

that in the wait, grown strict
in patience, we preserve
that softness for those so long
in wait behind the sail.

LOST, PERHAPS IN LONDON

She'd had the dream so many times
it was if that dream was what
her sleep was made for: being lost
where all the street names were the same,

one night stopping at a market
for directions, the next following
a stranger who assured where she
was was drinks away from danger.

That she was to meet someone was
a further constant, a colored
light she rounded every corner
hoping to see, to press her face

against the collar of a friendly
coat, to find whom she thought lost from
another dream that had not come
while sleeping, here now, though, in sleep,

content, at least, that in being
lost there was for now the chance of
finding that elusive sign that
pointed homeward, not for safety's

sake, nor for the face she would ever
see outside this vision, just trust
in an ephemeral promise
that the dream would not end but change.

NO WIT, NO SEX, NO MURDER

She stretches and shakes off the sleep
that has held her today until
mid-morning. This is not the way
life should have happened, she thinks,
her window a picture of new snow.

Maybe somewhere there was a man
who might have made a difference,
but if there was she never met him
or if she did she didn't think
so then, declaring the same old love.

If the weather weren't so bad, she
might drive over to Baxter Bridge—
there was something in the souvenir shop
she might get her mother for Christmas
and the owner there seemed comfortable.

If she didn't exist, someone
would have to make her up; she laughs
at being so ordinary that
a director couldn't use her even
in the crowd scene of a 50's plot.

Whatever it was that made life
interesting, she would like to know.
She guessed she'd trim the tree today;
and tomorrow, if the roads cleared,
buy a bottle (why not) of expensive wine.

WOMAN AWAY

The house is a creaking
of drying boards. I have
lit the front room and bedroom
fires, the pilot light for
the water heater in
the closet off the kitchen.

Outside, snow has begun
to stick on the fringes
of the road and on the sides
of maple and locust trees.

Such a welcome home,
returning to a house
that would embrace me had
it arms, my sister says.

Comfort is knowing there
are no timbers waiting here
to fall, no ghosts in walls
to protect a former owner:

it knows me, like the old
dog Lawrence used to have
that growled any night he
came home late, but never
raised its head at me.

Death wears a soft shoe here,
and when I die will step
a waltz, sweeping me a
beauty from the ball to his
dark door, to a room where
I’ll think I’ll want to go.

THE UNDESERVING

Where the tree holds against
the sky, night falls; you taught
us all, Marilyn, about
twilight, the rising of stars,

standing like Minerva
in your bold red and white,
one foot upon the world,
maddening us forever.

Indifferent to desire
we thought you were; your
indiscretions only
crazed us more, imagining
our hearts your trophies.

The tree holds against
the sky; if winter now,
we still stand in our stiff
watch, in our cold-clean clothes.

And whatever street we
cross, whatever mountain road,
we are drawn to your deep
mouth, to your wonder shoes.

PORTRAIT

Her hair is straight back, though we can't
tell from the photograph whether
or not it's in a bun. It is
a close up and she is alone,

which is unusual for pictures
of that time. We'll keep her relationship
to our family distant though
her resemblance to Sissy Spacek

must be more than coincidence
even if we must blot out later
the name of the actress lest our own
in future years seem too modern.

Not often comic or ironic,
if we are to trust ancestry
and her writings, she nevertheless
stood strong against her father's house

and never married, yet provided
gossip galore for townspeople
busy to bury their secret
diseases and homely children.

Anyway, there she is and you
can see how proud we are of her,
the way the eyes reveal neither
mischief nor malice, mouth pursed

and waiting for the inattentive
kinsmen's embrace, inviting
us to stand singularly faced
and immortal beside her.

FUNERAL

The light that kept
her fingers brown once
opens onto the beach,
across the dunes,
past the pines,

then stalls but a second
above the clearing
where a pitcher pump
and rusty cup
lie abandoned in weeds
beside a shed.

On the limbs
of the oak scrubs
roofing the road
leading in, dew hangs
before it unbuttons
to hundreds of
craters in the sand.

The light that made
her words day once
closes its hand and lies
down like the wind,

the weeds and tracks
and waves tucked
tightly in before
the great mountain.

DAWN MOUNTAIN FOG

It starts off as a dot
no bigger than a bug
the size of a flea on
a landscape painting I
remember from Munich.

I want to nudge it with
a pencil tip to see
if it's moving when the scene
changes and it's moving
all right, a shadow

using flat rocks to cross
the creek, then following
a path that disappears
behind a bluff of grass
before emerging again,

more ghostly than shadow,
more saintly than ghost,
head leaning, legs straining,
climbing into clothing,
until dwarfing the morning

she appears on the steps,
undoing her scarf,
shaking mist from her hair,
smiling and, hand on hip,
saying, See, here I am.

ALETHA

Scythe on shoulder, Time
comes to cut the meadow,
heavy pipe in mouth, smoking
Five Brothers tobacco.

Popping daisies, laying
clover in swaths, he will
not be done until he
mows the timothy too.

How you stood in yellow
dress in the swale of spring
beeches, what kind of flower
pinned sideways in your hair.

Now he stands gaunt, tilting
blade against whetstone, guarding
the glass jug of water
he has hidden in the grass.

Dusk, he will be finished,
curved snath on shoulder, deep
in dark woods awaited by
the king's own carriage.

How you made me ashamed
of my advances, your
face trembling, your eyes shy
enough to quiet deer.

www.ingramcontent.com/pod-product-compliance
Ingram Content Group UK Ltd.
Pitfield, Milton Keynes, MK11 3LW, UK
UKHW041315190726
13845UKWH00025B/278

9 789388 125840